Seal at the Wheel

Lesley Sims

Illustrated by David Semple

Seal gives a squeal.
She's seen a green sign.

For sale - one
speedboat
←

The speedboat is cheap.
She's aboard with a leap...

...honks the horn with her flipper.
"Let's go!"

With a spin of the wheel
Seal speeds from the bay.

She goes faster and faster.

"Eel! Out of my way!"

Hippo is wearing his new water skis.

Seal is scaring him.

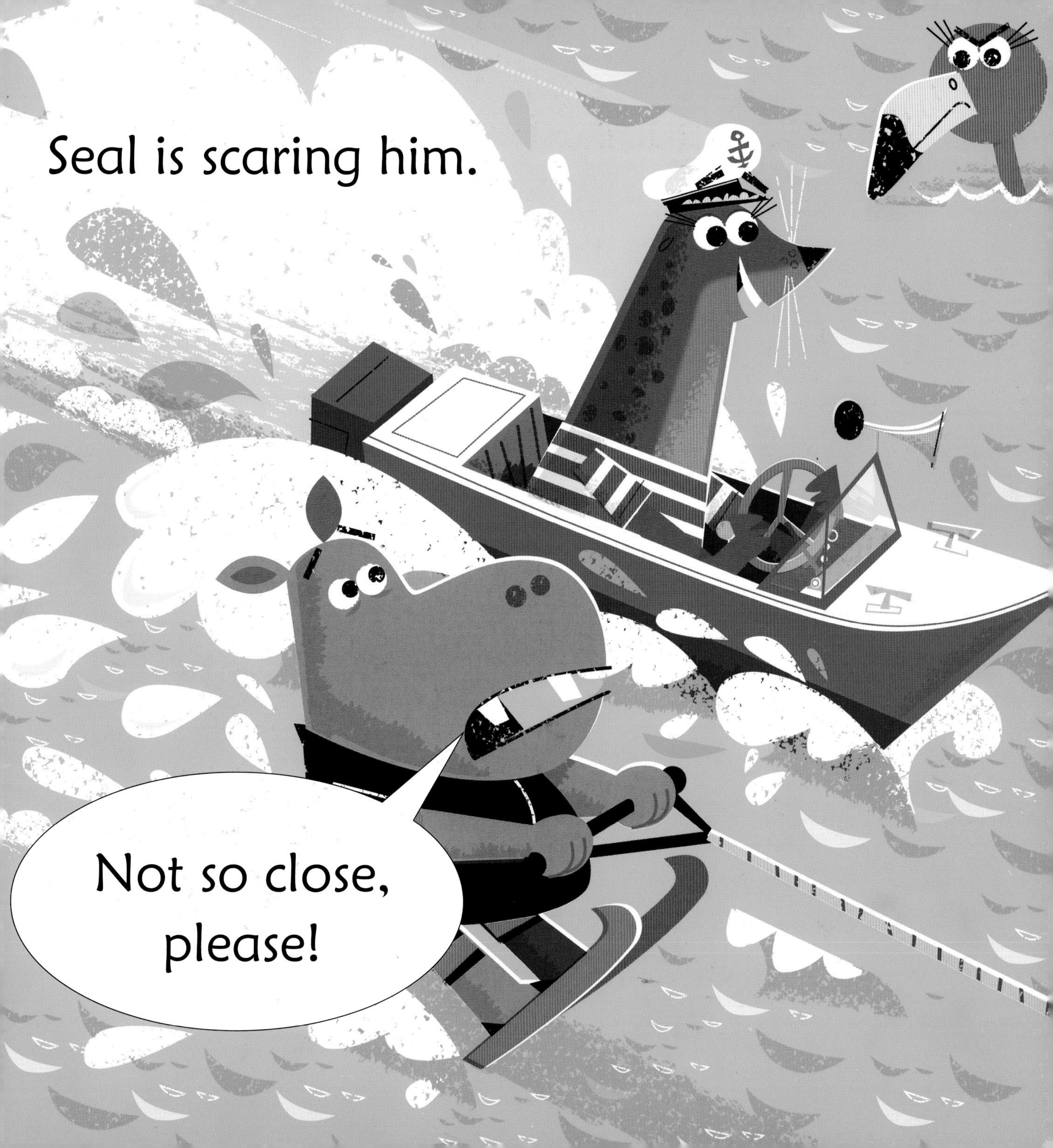

But Seal needs speed.
She is greedy for more.

She zips...

...Hippo flips

and he
surfs into
shore.

Seal's boat bounces wildly and bumps over waves

as she weaves up and down.

"Enough is enough!"
Hippo roars from the bay.

"You make the sea rough.
Seal, sail far away."

As Seal turns to leave...
a boat hits a rock.

Seal churns up the sea
as she speeds to the spot.

"Help! Our boat's leaking," some scared monkeys moan.

Seal hauls them to safety.

"I'll soon have you home."

Now Seal's still at the wheel,
speeding all round the bay.

She drives the town's lifeboat –
on call night and day.

About phonics

Phonics is a method of teaching reading used extensively in today's schools. At its heart is an emphasis on identifying the *sounds* of letters, or combinations of letters, that are then put together to make words. These sounds are known as phonemes.

Starting to read

Learning to read is an important milestone for any child. The process can begin well before children start to learn letters and put them together to read words. The sooner children can discover books and enjoy stories and language, the better they will be prepared for reading themselves, first with the help of an adult and then independently.

You can find out more about phonics on the Usborne Very First Reading website, **www.usborne.com/veryfirstreading** (US readers go to **www.veryfirstreading.com**). Click on the **Parents** tab at the top of the page, then scroll down and click on **About synthetic phonics**.

Phonemic awareness

An important early stage in pre-reading and early reading is developing phonemic awareness: that is, listening out for the sounds within words. Rhymes, rhyming stories and alliteration are excellent ways of encouraging phonemic awareness.

In this story, your child will soon identify the *ea/ee* sound, as in **leap** and **green**. Look out, too, for rhymes such as **zips** – **flips** and **skis** – **please**.

Hearing your child read

If your child is reading a story to you, don't rush to correct mistakes, but be ready to prompt or guide if he or she is struggling. Above all, do give plenty of praise and encouragement.

Edited by Jenny Tyler
Designed by Hope Reynolds

Reading consultants: Alison Kelly and Anne Washtell

First published in 2018 by Usborne Publishing Ltd., Usborne House, 83-85 Saffron Hill, London EC1N 8RT, England.
www.usborne.com Copyright © 2018 Usborne Publishing Ltd.